Tales of A Receding Hairline

K.W. Peery

GenZ Publishing

2015® K.W. Peery

ISBN: 978-0692613863

GenZPublishing.org

Aberdeen, NJ

DEDICATION

To Jen Anderson-Peery, my love and most trusted accomplice

Special Thanks To
Kenny Marshall, Andy Oxman, Bryant Carter,
Scott Ford & the Bourbon Brotherhood

Contents

ALONE

Standin' alone
In the pourin' rain
A hand full of sand
Is hard to explain
Forty-two years
More strife than struggle
Life's hard work
When your job is trouble

Standin' alone
Surrounded by faces
Hunted for sport
In the same sad places
Blue neon rooms
Born for sin
Where whiskey tells lies
And everyone's friends

Standin' alone

As the fire rages

A dog-eared book

With blood soaked pages

Nobody knows

The poets abuse

Bound by words

In a hangman's noose

ANCIENT EMBER

When an ancient ember lights a fire

In the chambers of your heart

Remember all the love you shared

Before the ragin' starts

Your lungs will simply feed the flames

More with every breath

When an ancient ember lights a fire

And your soul is scared to death

When an ancient ember lights a fire

And flesh starts to tingle

The depths of your restless gut

Is where good scotch goes to mingle

Burnin' more with every sip

Fingers against the glass

When an ancient ember lights a fire

And haunts you with your past

BONFIRE

A bonfire bleeds
Red, smoke and ash
While the soul still needs
Much more from its past
Timeless so tragic
In a pit of blue ember
Where a bonfire bleeds
At the edge of the timber

Where a bonfire bleeds
Pure loneliness reigns
Every night bitter
Stealin' more from the same
A hint of old hickory
Smells like home
Where a bonfire bleeds
It'll rattle your bones

K.W. Peery

BORN TO TROUBLE

She's the sound of old vinyl
On a cold, dark Winter night
Tastes just like a memory
The kind ya hope you can ignite

She's a stone white canvas
Beggin' for a drink
Everything ya need to know
And much deeper than you think

She was born to trouble
Under Tuesday's settin' Sun
With one foot on the dark side
Always on the run
She was born to trouble

She'll tempt you with her innocence

Her fire burns white hot

Everything ya wished you had

And all you better not

She's a high wire walker

Addicted to the show

Cheatin' death every night

She's trouble don't ya know

She was born to trouble

Under Tuesday's settin' Sun

With one foot on the dark side

Always on the run

She was born to trouble

CAPE

The voices South of Cape
Are hard to understand
So close to the fault line
You can hold the Devils hand
New Madrid in September
Will shake a restless soul
As the muddy water churns
The worry can take a toll

Somewhere North of Dyersburg
Buried in ancient sand
Are the skeletal remains
Of many a Bootheel clan
Hear their faded banjos
Haunt the Autumn breeze
With long crooked fingers
And bloody beech tree leaves

COLD

When the cold seeps in

On a midnight wind

And embers are all that's left

You'll tilt that bottle

More than ya oughta

As your veins try their best

Old ghosts dance

Over your last chance

Down on that hardwood floor

When the cold seeps in

On a midnight wind

And ya just hang no more

K.W. Peery

DARKNESS

Nobody knows the darkness

Quite like me

I'm addicted to rain

And cursed by the sea

Pullin' at my soul

It hurts when I breathe

Nobody knows the darkness

Quite like me

Sad songs and whiskey

When feelin' bad just ain't enough

Nobody knows the darkness

Or how I struggle...to give it up

Still tryin' to forgive myself

Lettin' go...is way too tough

Nobody knows the darkness

Or how I struggle...to give it up

Nobody knows the darkness

As well as I do

You can see it in my shadow

It's surrounded by the truth

Visceral reactions

Too often so uncouth

Nobody knows the darkness

As well as I do

DAYBREAK

Before the gold of daybreak

Where sunlight warms your face

You feel a hint of sorrow

From the sins you can't erase

A long walk through the timber

For a soul that can't let go

Before the gold of daybreak

Carryin' secrets ya never show

Before the gold of daybreak

Only truth left in your glass

Staring down both barrels

Praying the buzz will last

Trouble somehow finds you

As the depth of darkness leaves

Before the gold of daybreak

The only witnesses are the trees

Before the gold of daybreak

When your eyes are playing games

Ya swear you see her silhouette

Beyond the lighters flame

You hear a horned owl beckon

To the liar in your heart

Before the gold of daybreak

When your nerves just fall apart

Before the gold of daybreak

When hope bleeds in the air

You strangle your inner voice

After tying him to his chair

Troubled, torn and tragic

A victim of self-defeat

Before the gold of daybreak

Long after your guilt's asleep

DEVIL DOG

Standing out on the ragged edge

A Ka-Bar in his left hand

Red Man chew...beat black and blue

The Marines still in the man

Survived five trips to the combat zone

Nothin' will kill his trauma

His brand of pain...he can't explain

Not even to his Momma

Dog don't care what ya say

He just cares how you say it

So never mind...those words unkind

Bein' too nice...is overrated

Semper Fi...to the stars and stripes

A globe and anchor tattoo

The dog doesn't care what ya have to say

All the Hell he's been through

The VA...just turned him away

Said he makes too much money

Shrapnel, scars...twelve pins, three bars

No love for a broken Gunny

His second Wife split...took half his shit

When he was over in Afghanistan

Now it's Ramen noodles...toaster strudel

And Pabst Blue Ribbon cans

DIFFERENT

Dare to be different
As ya dual with death
Calculate risks
Then challenge yourself

Test the edge
Where no one will ride
Dare to be different
On the wilder side

Dare to be different
With your cape in the breeze
Leave them all guessing
And never say please

Embrace the journey
Reject the norm
Dare to be different
Tame the storm

Dare to be different
This time around
Flash the goods
Then take their crown

Nice to be King
In this land of plenty
Dare to be different
Paint life funny

DRIFTER

There's a gypsy in my shadow
Always tempting me
He sips on Booker's bourbon
And always seems so free

He owns a gold pocket watch
I've never seen him wind
There's a gypsy in my shadow
Who says I'll lose my mind

There's a rambler in my liver
That likes it when I drink
He loves to read Bukowski
While I piss in the kitchen sink

He seldom reads my poetry
Just heckles me from the crowd
There's a rambler in my liver
And his voice is way too loud

There's a drifter in my memory
Who knows the wrong I've done
He haunts me when I'm sober
And catches me if I run

Too many hidden pitfalls
For a man in my condition
There's a drifter in my memory
Who's waiting on my contrition

DRINKIN' IN THE RAIN

Standin' along the river's edge

Drinkin' in the rain

Water churns...as whiskey burns

Drownin' things he can't explain

Truth runs deep...where dead men sleep

Still searchin' for who's to blame

Standin' along the river's edge

Drinkin' in the rain

Drinkin' in the rain

Lyin' to himself

Wishin' he knew the answers

But the answers never help

Wonderin' where the words are

While smokin' his Brothers stash

Drinkin in the rain

Prayin this storm will pass

Standin along the river's edge

Skippin' flat rocks...gettin' stoned

Drinkin' in the rain

Weak signal on his phone

Might call if she'd answer

Their loves...on hold again

Drinkin in the rain

Until the bitter end

DUST

When dust finally settled

On the hurt ya left for dead

Everything felt kinda numb

Or at least that's what ya said

There was still a glimpse of misery

Held tight against your chest

When dust finally settled

And ya gasped for your last breath

When dust finally settled

Pants tucked down in your boots

With a half pint of whiskey

Heavy on the proof

Not much time for final rights

Defiant until the end

When dust finally settled

And the Angels led you in

DECEMBER RAIN

The rain in mid-December
Can soak a man down to his core
With everything he thought he knew
And just a little more
Water standin' in the blacktop grooves
As city lights fade away
The rain in mid-December
Tryin' to drown the Holidays

The rain in mid-December
Can wreck an old man's mind
Worryin' about the kind of things
He was not meant to unwind
Drivin' against the headlights glare
As his wipers try their best
The rain in mid-December
Howlin' Wolf and cigarettes

DYIN'

Traced my scars yesterday

In the middle of the afternoon

Then cracked a fifth of Jack

Knowin' Hell'd be callin' soon

I sat out on the front porch

Wishin' it would rain

There was lightnin' in the distance

But the rain...it never came

Brewed a pot of coffee

'Cause I like the way it smells

An early mornin' pick me up

When the last words start to fail

K.W. Peery

Wet ink on new paper

Empty bottles on the floor

A Blue Ribbon tragedy

That my liver can't help no more

Static on my radio

Just turned half past two

The Possum singin' somethin'

About leavin' what's left for you

Sleep is a dyin' outlaw

Elusive where he bleeds

Ain't no use in tryin'

Cause dyin' don't pay no heed

EARL

A Silvertone banjo
Pickin' the Muleskinner Blues
Crooked and crippled fingers
That his job made him abuse
Faded red bandana
Peekin' out from his bibs
A tattered shirt so thin
You could count his ribs

Some folks called him Earl
We just called him Pa
He moved from Oklahoma
Settled down in Arkansas
Eureka Springs took him in
Back in thirty-five
Some folks called him Earl
He's damn lucky he survived

The Dust Bowl made him crazy

In the midst of a Great Depression

Lost everything he owned

Except his lone obsession

Said music healed his soul

And the hills calmed his pain

Ozark Mountain Lightnin'

With Bluegrass in his veins

EASTER PAINTS

As Easter paints

The afternoon

He sits alone

In his living room

Deviled eggs

Communion wine

A hungry heart

And troubled mind

Heavy on lonesome

Boots on the floor

An old black cat

A green screen door

Too much truth

For a man to grasp

As Easter paints

His aftermath

Sun soaked skin

Warm Spring breeze

A garden of roses

On aching knees

Prayers for the fallen

Hymns for the hurt

As Easter paints

He tills the dirt

EIGHTY-ONE CUTLASS

An eighty-one Cutlass

With expired tags

Was sittin' on blocks

At my Girlfriend's Dads

It needed an engine

And was missin' some chrome

For a cool eight hundred

I took her on home

81 Cutlass

A silver Supreme

Built in the shade

When I was just sixteen

Blacktop roads

Warm Summer nights

An 81 Cutlass

With one tail light

Eighty-one Cutlass

Crude attitude

Put my hillbilly girl

In just the right mood

Her skinny long legs

In a worn back seat

Petty slow preachin'

Bout a Refugee

ELUSIVE

Still elusive

Runnin' free

If ya look right now

I don't look like me

Packin' heavy

To hide these scars

Rollin' the dice

Been livin' too hard

Still elusive

'Cause fame don't pay

At home in shadows

I love the fray

Tamin' all voices

Writin' what comes

It never slows down

I'm a Gatlin' gun

Still elusive

Rockin' silver temples

A sixty-eight Ford

I keep things simple

Nobody cares

To rattle this cage

The hound ran out

In my younger days

Still elusive

I'll take what comes

Forgiveness is futile

I'm the setting Sun

Like smooth on a Rosary

Before the grave

I can't drown out

My infamous ways

K.W. Peery

EMPTY

Hemorrhagin' words

Not meant for you

It's too late now

To speak the truth

Slide over here

And cast your spell

Hemorrhagin' words

I'll never tell

Bleedin' out slow

Down the back of my throat

I get so tired

At the end of this rope

Barely feel counted

Like a dead man's vote

Bleedin' out slow

Just buryin' hope

Life on tilt

Spillin' my booze

Never bought in

My game to lose

A thirty-eight special

On the passenger seat

Life on tilt

In the Ozark heat

Searchin' for empty

Full of myself

Dyin' inside

Won't ask for help

Pills and potions

Sick with rhymes

Searchin' for empty

And losin' my mind

END IN SIGHT

Almost outta bullets
Pinned against the wall
Everything we try to save
Sooner or later falls

As politicians pound their fists
With profits in both hands
War is Hell for the workin' man
Only few can comprehend

Is there an end in sight
Mission Accomplished was years ago
Afghanistan, the Taliban
No one really knows

As sand turns red, under severed heads
Where does the fair winds blow
Is there an end in sight...
No one really knows

Sniper fire ...and IED's

ISIS on the prowl

Do we fight or fade away

Too late to turn back now

Reactionary riddles

Solitary rhymes

CNN, Fox and Friends

Their rhetoric is a crime

For those so brave and fearless

Who suffer on broken wings

Warriors who've paid the ultimate price

Sacrificed everything

Questions deserve a better answer

Every wound needs relief

It's time for all Americans

To stop the doublespeak

K.W. Peery

FACES

Standin' out on Mission Beach
With the sand between our toes
It was the Nineties and Nirvana
Chili Peppers...and Ramones
Punk was really fadin' then...
But, we didn't fuckin' care
It was peace time...cheap red wine
When they cut off all my hair

Faces in the crowd
Every time I think of you
Down in San Diego
We were too young...to be true
Long before we figured out
Or learned about the blues

Faces in the crowd
Every time I think of you

I see faces in the crowd
Every time I think of you
A green Coleman cooler
Flip flops and Ray Ban shades
We would steal your roommates Beetle
Shit... we had it made
Cruise on out to that special spot
For high tide...on Point Loma
A far damn cry...from Friday night
In Hoot Owl Oklahoma

Faces in the crowd
Every time I think of you
Down in San Diego
We were too young...to be true
Long before we figured out
Or listened to the blues
Faces in the crowd
Every time I think of you

I see faces in the crowd
Every time I think of you

FOUR ROSES

Four Roses on his table

Shattered glass in a dirty sink

A wrinkle for every lie he's told

And for those nights he chose to drink

The poems he wrote at thirty

Are steadily collectin' dust

He's sure as hell...a little meaner now

Says there ain't no God he'd trust

Gave up speed at forty

When his heart...just couldn't hang

Four Roses on his table

Her hair cloggin' up the drain

She left him three months ago

Short note and a wedding band

Four Roses on his table

Says it's misery that breaks a man

Four Roses on his table

Butcher knife and a cuttin' board

Two green apples with peanut butter

Still loves ...ole Louis L'Amour

Says dyin' ain't the hardest part

Some livin'...is almost dead

Four Roses on his table

Never believed a word she said

FRAGMENTS

Fragments of mercy

Haunting the hurt

Everything open

Aching for dirt

Dipped in silver

Stripped by sin

Fragments of mercy

Again & again

Fragments of brilliance

Reflected pain

Healed by tragedy

Engulfed in flames

Vulnerable moments

Faces unnamed

Fragments of brilliance

Nothing's the same

Fragments of feeling

Bleeding your soul

A lifetime of lies

In a damned fish bowl

Clinical experts

Spiritual scholars

Fragments of feeling

Invisible squalor

GOOD FRIDAY

The mornin' Sun
Hurts his eyes
He drank too much
Late last night
Cinnamon and whiskey
Just don't mix
Voodoo charms
And guitar licks

Prayin' won't help
And the snakes no cure
Greasy fried fish
Last night's blur
Good Friday Mass
To confess all his sins
A fist full of dollars
No means to an end
Good Friday...
Oh yeah...it's Good Friday

The smell of incense

Burns his nose

Heads on fire

Wearin' last night's clothes

Dark sunglasses

Transfixed on a Hymnal

He feels kinda shaky

Needin' a signal

Prayin' won't help

And the snakes no cure

Greasy fried fish

Last night's blur

Good Friday Mass

To confess all his sins

A fist full of dollars

No means to an end

Good Friday...

Oh yeah...it's Good Friday

GRATEFUL

Grateful for forgiveness
As November fades away
Where all the leaves have fallen
With one foot in the grave

Nature shows no mercy
A Mother dressed in black
Grateful for forgiveness
On the wrong side of the tracks

Grateful for illusions
Beyond the headlight glare
Chasin' a last December
Where I'll surely drink my share

The blacktop looks like a skatin' rink
It shimmers of shattered glass
Grateful for illusions
And those not born to last

GROOVES

The grooves on this highway

Match the ones carved in my soul

And no matter how fast life gets

Miles can't make me old

The gristle that plagues a poet's heart

Can sometimes pump ice cold

And the grooves on this highway

Match the ones carved in my soul

The grooves in my pistol grip

Are for every man I had to kill

It's somethin' I'm not proud of

My wounds will never heal

War can shatter a fragile mind

Every shard is soaked in gas

The grooves in my pistol grip

Are for those not born to last

HER EYES

Her eyes are as wide

As a hurricane

Twistin' my thoughts

When I drown my brain

I don't wanna run

Cause it won't ease my pain

Yeah, her eyes are as wide

As a hurricane

Her eyes hold secrets

Against their will

Like shattered glass

On a windowsill

She'll cut ya deep

And send you the bill

Yeah, her eyes hold secrets

Against their will

Her eyes are trouble

It's hard to explain

At two in the mornin'

She's never the same

A handheld mirror

Three lines of cocaine

Yeah, her eyes are trouble

It's hard to explain

Her eyes of tomorrow

Are bleedin' today

Temptin' your soul

As she walks away

It's already over

When she begs ya to stay

Yeah, her eyes of tomorrow

Are bleedin' today

HUNTED

Hungry are the hunted

When the hunted are runnin' free

Alone with the wolves again

Who knows how long I'll be

Lines chopped out real crooked

Crucifix on the wall

Old Porter Wagoner records

Inherited from my Grandpa

At home with the lonesome

I dance in empty rooms

Hungry are the hunted

I know they're comin' soon

Turntable on a milk crate

Pistol in my waistband

Sorrow on the rocks

Harder hurt than I can stand

Hungry are the hunted

Just before the break of dawn

Too proud to fall asleep

And first to admit I'm wrong

Almost outta bourbon

Smoked up all my weed

Hungry are the hunted

When the hunted are huntin' me

HURT HELD HER

Hurt held her hand
On the Courthouse steps
Too many days
Not much left

Hell found her waitin'
And so did he
Hurt held her hand
Down in Tennessee

Hurt held her heart
Barbed wire -n- lace
You could see the miles
On her wrinkled face

It was two shots of bourbon

And Amazing Grace

Hurt held her heart

As it skipped in place

Hurt held her pieces

At the river's edge

She prayed for forgiveness

As her fingers bled

Scattered fragments

She'd left for dead

Hurt held her pieces

At the river's edge

JACK

A student of Woody Guthrie

New York... born and bred

A rodeo lovin' rambler

Cowboy hat on his ramblin' head

He inspired young Bob Dylan

Ole Jack still calls him...Son

South Coast...the Wild Coast

It's lonely son of a gun

The Cowboy from Brooklyn

Still ramblin along

For a nickels worth of whiskey

He'll sing you your favorite song

Flat pickin' and buskin'

From Tulsa... to Duson

The Cowboy from Brooklyn

Still ramblin' along

Still ridin' in his saddle

Some eighty-three odd years

He's rambled six lifetimes

And pinned back their goddamned ears

Bull Durham Sacks ... and Railroad tracks

Ole Jack...just rambles on

From London to Minneapolis

For the love of a real folk song

JOHNNY

They drafted ole John
At twenty-eight
Two babies at home
One on the way

It was Army green
With the Big Red One
A dagger tattoo
And a new machine gun

Johnny was tall...
And John was lean
When Johnny went to war
Ole John was mean

Hell haunted Johnny
At night in his dreams
Said the older he got...
The louder they screamed
Yeah, the older he got
The louder they screamed

Well Johnny made it home
Back to his Ruth
He drank and raised Hell
To hide from the truth
Johnny loved his family
From an arm's length away
And his soul held secrets
He took to the grave

Johnny was tall...
And John was lean
When Johnny went to war
 Ole John was mean

Hell haunted Johnny
At night in his dreams
Said the older he got...
The louder they screamed
Yeah, the older he got
The louder they screamed

KNOB CREEK BLUES

He built a big fire
On the outskirts of town
To burn some old love letters
He wished she'd never found

Drank rye whiskey
Then screamed out her name
Now truth lives in the ashes
Buried with the blame

Knob Creek Blues
Cursin' white hot flames
A three-day buzz
And a promise ring

The fire burned hot
With an old man's regret
Knob Creek Blues
Smokin' cheap cigarettes...

Knob Creek Blues and cheap cigarettes

His Seventy-Eight Chevy
Had four-wheel drive
The truck he drove
The night he took her life

He still keeps a picture
In the cracked sun visor
For nights he's haunted
And needs a reminder

Knob Creek Blues
Cursin' white hot flames
A three-day buzz
And a promise ring

The fire burned hot
With an old and man's regret
Knob Creek Blues
Smokin' cheap cigarettes...

The Knob Creek Blues ...and cheap cigarettes

KNOWING

Conscious incompetence

Shallow belief

Easier prey

Screaming sheep

Discounted virtue

Spoiling hope

Knowing is crystal

At the end of your rope

Worn and wrinkled

Hypocritical tongues

Talk more shit

Than Gatling gun

Conditional romance

Polished rust

Knowing is crystal

Just before the dust

Front row pew

On Sunday morning

Soaking it up

Even though it's boring

Illusion for sale

Rich pimp's cloth

Knowing is crystal

The longer you're lost

LAST NIGHT'S WINE

Last Night's Wine
Still hurts today
An overcast sky
Nothin' to say
A long trip home
When the wind won't lay
And Last Night's Wine
Still hurts today

Last night's wine
Sure tasted good
A Red Zinfandel
In aged oak wood
Portuguese Port
More than I should
Last Night's Wine
Sure tasted good

Last Night's Wine

In an old dancehall

Drunk on love

A masquerade ball

Amplified strings

Raw Fender squall

Last Night's Wine

In an old dancehall

Last Night's Wine

To celebrate Fifty

A milestone smile

Still needs to feel risky

Front man swagger

With a cool intensity

Last Night's Wine

To celebrate Fifty

LAST

Thirsty for the silence

When noise is all that's left

Angrier now than I have to be

Too tired for a peaceful rest

Hard booze in a coffee cup

Early mornin' rain

Thirsty for the silence

The voices are soundin' strange

Hungry for forgiveness

When I can't take it back

Somewhere along the highway

Old tires on shattered glass

Miles ...they stack up quickly

In the groove... spinnin' fast

Hungry for forgiveness

I'm bound finish last

ILLUSION

Beautiful pain

Magnificent hurt

If ya choose to feel

The loneliness works

Drunk with illusion

Stoned on goodbye

Ya can't see the Sun

For the tears in your eyes

Grasping for somethin'

Beyond the Blue Moon

Aching for nothin'

A needle and spoon

Thirteen Luckys

Some black cat bones

It's all an illusion

When nobody's home

LIMITS

He pushes the limits

Every now and then

Drinks white lightnin'

Where the black top ends

Takes too long

To call it a day

So ya best steer clear

Of his Chevrolet

Has a three fifty bored

With sixty over

He pushes the limits

When he's feelin' older

A nineteen eleven

Ed Brown carry

An Ozark curse

His edge is scary

He pushes the limits

To rattle your cage

It's too late now

For his soul to be saved

Dust on the Bible

Hell on his breath

A crossroads smirk

He ain't dead yet

Rattle can paint

On the passenger door

Where he pushed the limits

Just a little more

Scars on his knuckles

Sand in his soul

Pushin' the limits

Till it's time to fold

LINES

Erasin' the lines
On a fractured mirror
Wantin' her back
But can't quite see her
Head on fire
Holdin' gasoline
Erasin' the lines
Is killin' me

Erasin' the lines
I walked for a while
Cranked up now
Like a radio dial
Early AM
Classic Country Gold
Erasin' the lines
I'm feelin' old

Erasin' the lines

Where the boundaries were

Hundred miles an hour

In a blenders blur

Tortured windshield

Four bald tires

Erasin' the lines

Underneath my smile

Erasin' the lines

Just an empty shell

Deal done made

This side of Hell

Half spent fifth

Thirsty for more

Erasin' the lines

Huggin' the floor

Erasin' the lines

Invisible now

Tryin' real hard

Forgot somehow

Forty-two years

Done came and went

Erasin' the lines

My luck got spent

MIDNIGHT IN CALIFORNIA

Midnight in California
Already two in Tennessee
And everything that broke her heart
She gave back to me

Twenty-Two...feelin' used
At a pay phone in Palm Springs
Midnight in California
Already two in Tennessee

Midnight in California
Spent bottle on a dirty floor
Next to a Wynette record
She couldn't listen to no more

Crooked lines on a mirror
She tried hard to ignore
Midnight in California
Spent bottle on a dirty floor

It was midnight in California
Heartbreak without the Petty
At the Cadillac Motel
I think she drove a Chevy

Tears shattered the silence
When she thought I was ready
Midnight in California
Heartbreak without the Petty

Midnight in California
Where our love went to die
A cool late December
I think it was Ninety-Five

I'll never forget the pain I felt
That night she took her life
Midnight in California
Where our love went to die

NORTH FOR SUMMER

As birds fly North for Summer
An old plow breaks new ground
There's fresh hope born at daybreak
On the outskirts of my hometown

Nobody thinks it's easy
But, everyone's sure they could
Most wouldn't last an hour
In my rural neighbourhood

No gang signs or graffiti
Just tobacco and diesel fuel
As birds fly North for Summer
Folks don't sit out by the pool

Where hay bales look like Tiki huts
Scattered across our land
You can soak your feet in Parsons Creek
Or run lines down on the Grand

No half ass country outlaws
Makin' good don't require crime
As birds fly North for Summer
Above the Mason Dixon line

Somewhere on a tractor
The Sunset paints the sky
As birds fly North for Summer
There's a damn good reason why

NUMBER EIGHT TURQUOISE

Number Eight Turquoise
Saddlebags filled with silver
A painted horse named iron
Six miles South of Denver

Revenge in his rifle
Loaded to kill the pain
A Bushwhacker from Missouri
Headed out on the Western Plains

Wicked don't quite cut it
He was death in dusty clothes
Number Eight Turquoise
A scar across his nose

Peacemaker plated nickel
Nerves forged in steel
Twelve crooked notches
For every man he had to kill

Snatched twelve gold nuggets

From a huckster in Cheyenne Wells

Number Eight Turquoise

Just sent him straight to Hell

The Lawmen formed a Posse

To chase the elusive beast

Down to Royal Gorge

Where he put them all to sleep

His legend has many versions

Most just half assed fiction

In the chronicles of time

He's folklore's lost edition

Never another like him

Many died pretending

Number Eight Turquoise

The book without an ending

OPEN WINDOWS

I walk past open windows
Achin' for the rain
And every time clouds build up
The wind decides to change

Elusive...blue horizon
Still thirsty for a storm
I walk past open windows
Fragile and forlorn

I walk past open windows
Here on the thirteenth floor
Almost outta courage
Could handle a little more

This hurt...it holds no mercy
For a poet near the end
I walk past open windows
Still searchin' for a friend

LONESOME

Lonesome's never tortured me

The way it did last night

Standin' at the threshold

With the soft, warm candlelight

Knowin' nothin' could bring her back

Despite how hard I tried

Lonesome's never tortured me

The way it did last night

Lonesome's never haunted me

This much in late November

Wide awake at 2AM

Just stirrin' the dyin' embers

One more splash in a dirty glass

For the hurt down in my bones

Lonesome's never haunted me

Since I've been alone

OUT IN THE OPEN

Standin' out in the open
Vulnerable and unscathed
Soul still searchin' for somethin'
More than itself to save

Where black dirt holds the answers
For questions you'll never ask
Standin' out in the open
Wishin' ya wore your mask

Standin' out in the open
With the unvarnished truth
While a fire inside you beckons
They threaten your ancient roots

A fine line emerges
With faces from yesterday
Standin' out in the open
Where there's nothin' left to say

OVER

Where will I be when it's over
How will I feel as I fade
When does this journey have meaning
Who am I trying to save

What will the truth unravel
When will my sins find release
Where will I be when it's over
Do I deserve to find some peace

Is mercy reserved for believers
Does this cross hold magical powers
Where will I be when it's over
Who will call in my final hours

Will Guardian Angels surround me
Can I travel well beyond this realm
Where will I be when it's over
And who will stand at the helm

PARTS UNKNOWN

Grand River in the Winter

Is a place I like to go

Carryin' a pint of misery

No need for a fishin' pole

Where sorrow begs forgiveness

And the wind...she blows so cold

Grand River in the Winter

Ancient truths there to behold

The back roads of Linn County

Is where I like to drive

If I make it through December

I'm damn lucky to be alive

With Haggard on cassette tape

In my Seventy Chevrolet

The back roads of Linn County

Where most the good times stay

A Lonesome Country Church

On the outskirts of parts unknown

Is where my Grandpa prayed for me

When I went out on my own

Today it sits abandoned

The yard still filled with bones

A Lonesome Country Church

Among the places I like to roam

PILE

There's a pile of busted screen doors
At the bottom of my mind
Rusted there together
That I tried to leave behind

Too many nights of lonely
Ridin' on the late night breeze
There's a pile of busted screen doors
And more that wait for me

There's a pile of shattered Mason jars
That took some time to kill
Holes so deep and hollow
My crazy could never fill

Starin' across this pasture

As the Sun is sinkin' slow

There's a pile of shattered Mason jars

Where the muddy water flows

There's a pile of rusted rifle brass

At the base of an old hedge post

Six miles East of Hecla

Just off Argo Road

Where yesterday begs forgiveness

And regrets all that's left

There's pile of rusted rifle brass

And the hurt won't let me rest

PILLS & BLOOD

Pills and blood

On the bathroom floor

He purged his soul

So he could die some more

The bourbon couldn't fix

What time can't change

So he punished his heart

And tortured his veins

Pills and blood

On the kitchen floor

He cooked a batch

So he could crank some more

The speed felt better

Than ownin' the blame

Up all night

Playin' video games

Pills and blood

On a cracked storm door

Where they slammed his head

Before he hit the floor

Dirty deeds

Are hard to survive

Three hollow points

From a forty five

Pills and blood

Are all he left

His neighborhood

Still hooked on meth

Wicked smiles

Through front porch screens

Sellin' new lies

And killin' old dreams

QUESTION EVERYTHING

I still question everything

My scars show where I've been

I prefer to remain eccentric

No need for a bunch of friends

I love days when I'm left alone

Cause the silence knows me best

I still question everything

For the most part I am blessed

Channelin' strangers' voices

Wide awake at 3AM

I still question everything

Over and over again

Most say I'm an asshole

To the jealous...I don't exist

I still question everything

And expose the hypocrites

I still question everything

It's certain I always will

My veins are filled with caffeine

No need for designer pills

Pushin' my forties into a ditch

Who knew I'd last this long

I still question everything

In search of a better song

REFLECTIONS

Reflections in the water
Remind me that you're gone
And everything I wish I'd said
Somehow lingers on
Forgiving you was easier
Than any hurt I tried drown
Reflections in the water
Faded love in a wedding gown

Reflections on carnival glass
Traced by candlelight
I can feel your spirit with me
Almost every night
At this lonesome kitchen table
I'll craft another line
Reflections on carnival glass
Purple hues & Native Wine

PAINTED WINGS

She painted on her wings
With an old bamboo brush
While he sat in the corner
Wishin' she wouldn't paint so much
Mixed with blue illusion
And silver in her hair
She painted on her wings
Then vanished in thin air

The breeze that night was sweeter
As he held his hurt inside
She painted on her wings
Then gently waved goodbye
For almost fifty years
The two remained as one
She painted on her wings
When her masterpiece was done

SHATTERED

Shattered on the bottom

Left to die at Sea

Moments before the walls caved in

Somethin' washed all over me

Hard to explain how deep it was

No one could hear me scream

Shattered on the bottom

Somewhere in between

Shattered on the ragged edge

Where writers go to die

Minutes before discovery

Too worn to question why

Time had come with the mornin' Sun

In the end...it's pale blue sky

Shattered on the ragged edge

Still learnin' how to fly

Shattered near the railroad tracks

On a bed of white hot cinders

A paper sack...with Old Grand Dad

Strung out on another bender

Harmonica buzz...coal car dust

Soul stuck in a blender

Shattered near the railroad tracks

On the thirteenth of November

SHE

She handed me a Rosary

She had tucked down in her purse

Said it's saved an ass once or twice

Wanna see if it still works

Her hands were worn and fragile

Every vein had its place

She handed me a Rosary

In a moment I can't erase

She prayed for me on Sunday

And every sleepless night

With Blue Kerosene

She was the keeper of the light

At times I'm sure she struggled

To invent new reasons why

She prayed for me on Sunday

With tears welled up inside

She saved me at the bottom

Where losers go to die

Said it's never the fall that kills ya

It's the lies ya just can't hide

Don't duel with darkness

Where only the truth survives

She saved me at the bottom

And I couldn't believe my eyes

SILENCE

Silence waits

To drink you in

Behind the curtain

With a crooked grin

Slicked back hair

An old guitar

The silence waits

Wherever you are

Silence waits

As the stage lights burn

Always on edge

For the closers turn

Seldom a profit

When they pay in cash

Silence waits

For the aftermath

SHADOWS

Where shadows dance on gravel
Just beyond the railroad tracks
Graffiti cars cast their sparks
As I drink from a paper sack

This poet lost at midnight
Both hands off the wheel
Where shadows dance on gravel
And sorrow is all I feel

Where shadows dance on gravel
Down a lonesome rural road
Tomorrow holds no guarantees
The truth sure takes a toll

This writer shares no answers
More questions come with age
Where shadows dance on gravel
Someplace beyond the grave

SOMETIMES

Sometimes she'll let you see her

Before November calls

Her silhouette...is not settled yet

Especially in the Fall

It's a one lane road...where tall grass grows

The trees look like crooked fingers

Oh, sometimes she'll let you see her

On those days her perfume lingers

Sometimes she'll let you chase her

Out across an open field

So ya run in place...with a determined face

And pray for faster wheels

At the edge of the timber...where yesterday splinters

She vanishes in thin air

Oh, sometimes she'll let you chase her

When she convinces you she's there

SUNDAY MORNIN'

Woke up Sunday mornin'

Made my way to the bathroom sink

Started to shave for church

Knowin' at church I wouldn't drink

Waitin' for communion

Last night's whiskey on my breath

I woke up Sunday mornin'

Prayin' Lord don't take me yet

Grandpa's Bible ridin' shotgun

Third pew...on the left

I woke up Sunday mornin'

With a pressure in my chest

Head poundin'...eyes bulgin'

Wrinkled shirt & muddy jeans

Yeah, I woke up Sunday mornin'

Stuck somewhere in between

SUNDAY SINS

Washin' Sunday Sins

Three fingers at a time

Chasin' elusive ghosts

Folks say are in my mind

The moral of the story

Is life can be unkind

So I'm washin' Sunday Sins

Three fingers at a time

Washin' Sunday Sins

Soakin' in the rain

As lightnin' paints the sky

My heart pumps more pain

This hurt feels like a hammer

As it pounds my ragin' brain

I'm washin' Sunday Sins

Standin' out in the rain

Washin' Sunday Sins

Makin' up reasons why

The Lord left me here

While my Brothers had to die

Torture has many faces

Seems evil don't have to try

I'm washin' Sunday Sins

And makin' up reasons why

Washin' Sunday Sins

Where only the shattered fall

Beggin' for forgiveness

Watin' on my call

 Nobody loves the broken

Our truth is all too raw

Washin' Sunday Sins

Where only the shattered fall

TEQUILA

She drinks straight tequila

When old flames won't let her rest

Don Julio Blanco

Wicked edge in a new red dress

Says Forty-One ain't easy

When leavin's all that's left

She drinks straight tequila

When old flames won't let her rest

She drinks straight tequila

On lonesome Monday nights

Listenin' to Waylon Jennings

When her wrongs aren't dyin' right

Three fingers for the misery

Always rarin' for a fight

She drinks straight tequila

On lonesome Monday nights

She drinks straight tequila

'Because she likes the way it feels

Long after closin' time

Kicked off her goodbye heels

Hooker...stoned on vinyl

For blues that are all too real

She drinks straight tequila

Cause she likes the way it feels

THE DARKNESS

There's somethin' within the darkness

Just minutes before daylight

Where everything runs scared

And your senses don't feel right

On edge...near big timber

You can hear the wicked scream

There's somethin' within the darkness

That's chasin' you in your dreams

There's somethin' within the darkness

That's beggin' you to stay

It wants to pull ya under

So you can't get away

Temptin' you with trinkets

Promisin' a brighter Moon

There's somethin' within the darkness

That's been savin' an extra room

SUNSET

Where the Sunset swaggers

Engulfing your day old pain

The sky will cheat a foolish heart

With beauty ya can't explain

As waves wash the words away

Ya wrote while drinkin' rum

The Sunset swaggers

And everything feels numb

Where the Sunset swaggers

And mercy don't know your name

Ya run on fumes again

Dancin' closer to the flames

Ya hear a voice so distant

That listenin' won't do no good

Where the Sunset swaggers

A little more than it should

TWENTY BELOW

Jerry Jeff records
Usually cheer me up
But, tonight I'm thinkin'
It won't be enough
She's somewhere in Memphis
I'm here in the snow
And this side of Hell
It's twenty below

Pot belly stove
Her note on the table
Single barrel whiskey
Has a prettier label
As I sit here and listen
The deeper it burns
It's twenty below
With every lesson I learn

Twenty-four carat

In an opal cut

Long skinny fingers

Crossed for luck

Her lipstick smudge

On a Sunny Delight

It's twenty below

And I'm here all night

WAKE UP FORTY

Ya wake up forty
Broke and alone
Wish you were famous
But your covers been blown
Crossroads callin'
Nobody cares
Fried chicken grease
And a black cats stare

Double barrel shotgun
Next to the bed
A dirty lampshade
Hand painted red
The smell of her perfume
Mixed with regret
Ya feel the end comin'
But it's not there yet

Ya wake up forty

Clothes on the floor

Twelve pill bottles

Still hungry for more

Head on fire

Hell on your breath

Smolderin' ashes

Anyone's guess

Four crooked lines

On a hot pink mirror

Credit card chalk

Cause faster is clearer

Like flickering neon

A poet gets gassed

Alone with the voices

Refusin' to last

THREE WOLVES

Three wolves wait

For your hurt to ease

Deep in the timber

Neath a big oak tree

Throats so dry

Their jaws gone stiff

Hungry and waitin'

To catch a sniff

Three wolves wait

For your last move

In late September

You're bound to lose

Steady hands tremble

As the flask goes dry

Three wolves wait

Till they see your eyes

Tales of a Receding Hairline is a GenZ™ Publishing Book

GenZ™ is an innovative publishing platform for the new generation to have their work seen, recognized, published and read by millions. When an individual is chosen to be published on GenZ™, they can use that experience in their portfolios, for résumés, to share with friends, family, and fans. It is an accomplishment to be proud of for the rest of their lives.

We are on a mission to improve the world one word at a time. That is why we are the place for voices to be heard in a way not previously done in print and on digital media. It is a way to support young writers, our new voices.

It can be nearly impossible for young writers with promising talent to produce standout work that will be recognized, because of the state of the publishing and digital media industries. Having work recognized in a sea of so many writers is even tougher. That is why there is an underrepresentation of young and innovative voices in the publishing and print world. There are many unheard voices. GenZ is on a mission to change that.

GenZ™ provides a medium where these people can be positively recognized for their work through a professional product and supportive company.

Learn more about GenZ Publishing, how you can get involved, and all of our newest releases at GenZPublishing.org. Like us on Facebook at GenZ Publishing and follow us on Twitter @GenZPub.

K.W. Peery

Printed in Great Britain
by Amazon